The Goodbye Child

By

Dominique Traverse Locke

ISBN-13: 978-0615642000 (Aldrich Publishing)

Aldrich Publishing Company
1840 West 220th Street Suite 300
Torrance, Ca. 90501

Acknowledgments

Grateful acknowledgment is made to the editors of the following journals where many of these poems were originally published, a few in different versions:

SEX originally appeared in Pine Mountain Sand & Gravel and was originally titled BERRY PICKING, 2012

BEDTIME STORY originally appeared in Howl, 2011

THE GOODBYE CHILD originally appeared in The Dead Mule, 2011

THE ORANGE FACES originally appeared in Jimson Weed, 2011

STORIES I TELL originally appeared in The Dead Mule, 2011

BY WINTER originally appeared in Referential Magazine, 2012

THE MISCARRIAGE CIRCUS originally appeared in Barely South Review, 2012

BLUE RIBBON originally appeared in Barely South Review, 2012

NIGHT POEM originally appeared in The Sow's Ear Poetry Review, 2012

For Dad and Mom,
and for David

Table of Contents

Poetry

Blue Ribbon

I don't like to brag but I grow the best
death and heartache of anyone around.
You might say I have a black thumb,
a knack for homegrown agony.
Last summer, I planted a child and a father
in the same row, just days apart. I weeded them
and showered them with a watering can
I kept behind my eyes.
My harvest won *Best Suffering* at the county fair.
It even beat the jelly made from bruises.

After the Miscarriage

How could those fireflies
whose wings opened into
a black V, snatched from the air
by my small glowing fingers
flicker back into my life,
so many nights later
in a neon green dream?

By Winter

By late July,
the pastureland
glows golden. The hay is
belly-button high,
ready to be cut
and dried for a second time
this year.
Muddy pawed rabbits
tunnel underneath, sensing
the imminent harvest.

By mid-August,
the corn is tall and heavy with
plump shucks of milky kernels,
a trellis for half-runners,
blue lakes, and yellow wax beans.
Yesterday, the neighbor's lost cow
stomped through the cucumbers
on her way to the cabbage.
Today, I hear the repairing
of locust posts.

I breathe deep and notice
the vines already withering,
the earth cracking dry.
I will be, by winter, fatherless.

Harvest

                                 I want to accept the end
of summer without accepting the death of my father.
        I taste the word, roll it around on my tongue:
Autumn.
        I see the pumpkins, the mums, the Indian corn at the market.
        The first orange leaf ignites on its branch

and the world goes up in red and gold.

The Orange Faces

I rummaged through the vines until I found one for each of us
and limped with the weight of them from the garden to the porch.
Late into that night, I sat scooping gut and seed from their insides.
The newspapers went soggy.
The air cold.
                                        I tried to carve regular faces.
Features suited to the shape and spirit of each pumpkin.
Toothy grins, nostrils, triangle eyes.
But when I lit the little candles and fixed the lids over the flames,
neither of them smiled.

Cancer Poem

I.

How easy life is
on the toilet each morning,

and the six or seven times
I return there each day.

And feeling such guilt
that I can do it

without help,
without tubes and bags

the way he did
his last two years.

II.

When I got home,
he was standing

in the bathroom
pulling the draw

string tight and
the pants still

swallowed his
ever diminishing body.

The Goodbye Child

My love, my tenant, you hardly existed.
But I thought I saw you. It was night, and you were there
in the doorway – a little girl, dark hair pulled back
with a ribbon like a puritan, a yellow square shining
behind you. But the change came all at once. Red,
and you were gone. I grieved for you then,
as I had never done before.

Reading Interrupted

I walk naked from the bathroom,
leaving a white, humid outline of each foot behind
on my way to you. You're in my bed again,
reading again, but stop as I unravel
the towel from my hair. I watch your eyes.
You watch my nipples stiffen.
Already, I am drying in the air between us.
Face down, the open book holds your page.
My breasts flatten against your chest.

Sex

The raspberries hang heavy,
swollen on their fuzzy stems
and I spend the morning
reaching arms, striped
with scratches, back
through brambles and briars
to snatch the deep red
honey of summer.

Stores I Tell

You listen to them.
The ones that come in short bursts and the ones that drag on
into the evening, night, morning.
My brother and the fish story.
My father and the cancer story.

Sometimes you ask questions
and I watch your Adam's apple rise up in your throat
the way a cork moves up the wet neck of a bottle of pale yellow wine.
I study your lips. The way they shape the air.
The sheer mechanics of your strong jaw.
Your spongy tongue.

And when you stop, I answer.
But what I want to do is fall to my knees,
crawl all the way to some holy place
to thank God for creating a voice,
unhurried and burning,
a soft coal in the stove of my soul.

Lament

I always look at the black and
white children hanging
from push pins on bulletin boards, knowing
most of them would not return.
So yesterday when I lost you,
I didn't waste time
tacking flyers onto the walls of my womb.

Lost in Our Home, a Dream

I was doing laundry,
mine and yours.
We had known of our shared life
for only a few months,
yet I stood there snapping out wrinkles
from your faded khaki slacks and folding
my favorite pajamas.
I left a pile of socks on the dryer's top for you.
Even in this world,
I hated matching them.
You were in the kitchen. Your voice,
distant and coffee coated, called to me.
Still new to this house,
I opened many doors before finding my way to you.

Night Poem

You spoke to me last night, while sleeping.
Said things plain and loud. I knew
I should make myself get up,
find the black and white notepad
you place in your pocket before work each day.
Write your message down. But I was exhausted
from weeding and mulching the flowerbeds,
bent over in the sun pulling this, scattering that.
      You kept proclaiming your prophecy
all through the night, waking me, then lulling me
back to sleep. It is then, in that soft silence,
the dew gathering on the lilies,
that what we don't say saves us.

Bedtime Story

I pat my lap and the moon sits down.
It is difficult to describe, I say to the moon.
There is a moment of strange calm
when you realize you are no longer a mother.
Not that the moon understands, ever faithful
in its roundness, unlike my stomach, flat
as the line of the little once upon a time heartbeat.

Leaving

In bed this morning, emptiness I didn't want
to see. And in your absence, I remembered
how you traced the outline of my face
with kisses and wedged your knee between my thighs.

How you and I enveloped each other
into late afternoon, early evening,
letting time settle all around us
and we still had hours.

The Miscarriage Circus

I.

He had an elephant between his legs.
That's what he wanted the audience to believe
when he entered the Big Top riding a worm
underneath a gray sheet, while the other clowns squirted
each other with hoses.

II.

When the tightrope walker took the spotlight,
she was naked except for the pink tutu
squeezing her waist. The pole, heavy in her hands, dictated
each step. Her body in the middle of the wire, toes pointed,
could sense only that there was no net,
no net beneath.

III.

The fat man with a mustache and top hat yells
Come one, come all and take a look at the unformed thing!
The strange little creature with no face, no bones!
The crowd races to enter the tent and gathers around
a glass jar of alcohol – a bean-shaped boy floats inside.

Eating Together

I.

A quick jab with the end tine punctures the yoke –
its jaundiced fluid spills over shredded hash browns.
He leans across the booth for a napkin.

He wipes away crumbs from his fingertips,
and packs his cheeks full of egg and toast.
Every time he eats, he feeds *it* too.

II.

I sat beside him, solicitous,
slipped into his mouth
bits of peaches –

his last meal,
soft and sweet
on his tongue.

Too Much

The meatloaf and fried chicken
showed up in the black sleeved arms
and throw away foil pans
of the neighbors. I felt sorry for the
kitchen table, buried
deeper, already,
than my father.

In Line

This afternoon, a two year old,
maybe three,
screams his miniature guts out.

Instead of wishing for a dirty sock
and bandana to gag him,
I envy him.

How he lets his anger pour
from his throat and eyes.
The precision of his little flailing arms.

I wish I could drill into my own fields of ache,
strike sadness and celebrate it.
How long would I have to sob

before the lady by the apples hands me a tissue,
or the man behind me offers his shoulder?
How many times must I wipe my eyes

before another shopper joins in?
Soon the cashier hunched over the register,
the manager counting the money,

the entire store will become a quivering box
with a glass sliding door.

The Second Wife

When I awoke, bitter and cursing
that glass of water, I kissed you
as you lay in the most silent moments,
and told you that I'd be right back, and pulled
the covers up to keep the heat. You took
a deep breath, and scratched your nose
with the back of your hand, then mumbled
We've had a good run, haven't we?
I left the bedroom, dodging carefully
our dogs and cats, wondering
who you had been running with or away from.
Your first wife? Me?
                        I rinsed my hands,
dried them on what was once her towel,
and came back to you with so many questions,
which is to say, only one question
that needed an answer. And so
I slinked back in next to you, trying
to break some kind of code,
and you seemed yourself unchanged.

Suicide

When grief woke me this morning,
I realized how a woman might select
her own death as easily as finding
a tall sunflower in a field of
white daisies.

Leaving the Nest

We never sat down and passed the potatoes like those good families.
We each grabbed on the run, mouths too full to talk
of the day. And now, I sit in my own kitchen, scraping
the jar's bottom for peach preserves – your last taste of Earth. There,
on top of the biscuit, I see the same deep brown of your eyes.
At the head of the table, I set a place for you. Above the absence,
the window reveals a crow perched above a weathered nest,
an empty cradle wafting in the tree.

After My Father's Diagnosis, a Haiku

My darling mother,
the poor hypochondriac,
has prostate cancer.

Open Window

Night is singing its night song.
Crickets, frogs, the hoot owl.
The mute purple of the sky
meets the black grasses in the field.

A woman who can't sleep
catches fireflies with her eyes.
Her unborn's death rests
in the long limbs of the willow.

A friend said that it's better
to have someone there waiting on you.

The woman imagines her child chasing
the blinking glow, lighting up the dark
with a toothfairy grin.

Living, she thinks, is the night song.
The wind whispers a lullaby,
and she sleeps.

Steeping Silence

This is when it happens.
Waking early, when the house holds no surprises,

and I find myself alone inside my own walls.
And the first sun rises over the first ridge, lighting carefully

the first trees from bottom to top.
The first bird cries out on the first morning,

and I am alone, and much of what is left
of my life will be this way.

Half orphaned, until my mother dies too.

Quiet

The lost ones are like that,
so careful not to bother the living.

Can something be made from this pain?
I have stitched together a blanket from its pieces.

I would have wrapped you in this blanket,
closed your tiny eyes with kisses, and each night,

scraped the dark from my face to watch you sleep.
I would have given up dreaming to keep watching.

Now, the days pass by. Good days, but many of them
I miss us being one body, mothering blood and bone.

About the Author

Dominique Traverse Locke received her B.A. in English from Virginia Intermont College in 2006 where she served as editor of the college's literary magazine, and received her M.F.A. in Creative Writing from Queens University of Charlotte. While at Queens, Dominique studied with Cathy Smith Bowers, Pinckney Benedict, Alan Michael Parker, Robert Polito, Sally Keith, Claudia Rankine, and many other fine masters of their craft. She has been publishing work in regional literary magazines such as *Barely South Review*, *The Sow's Ear Poetry Review*, and many other fine publications regularly since 2006. She resides in the Appalachian Mountains of southwest Virginia with her husband, the poet, David Alan Locke.